FACTS AMERICA

THE
CIVIL WAR

ERIC WEINER

zigzag

About the author

Eric Weiner is the author of 14 fiction and nonfiction books for children. He was a staff writer for Nickelodeon's Ace Award-winning television series "Eureeka's Castle" and has won two Edpress Awards for his children's magazine writing.

Editor:
Philip de Ste. Croix

Designer:
Stonecastle Graphics Ltd

Picture research:
Leora Kahn

Coordinating editors:
Andrew Preston
Kristen Schilo

Production:
Ruth Arthur
Sally Connolly
Neil Randles
Andrew Whitelaw

Production editor:
Didi Charney

Director of production:
Gerald Hughes

Typesetter:
Pagesetters Incorporated

Color and monochrome reproduction:
Advance Laser Graphic Arts, Hong Kong

Printed and bound in China
by Leefung-Asco Printers Ltd

This edition published in 1997 by Zigzag Publishing,
a division of Quadrillion Publishing Ltd. Godalming Business
Centre, Woolsack Way, Godalming, Surrey GU7 1XW

Distributed in the U.S. by SMITHMARK PUBLISHERS
a division of U.S. Media Holdings, Inc.
16 East 32nd Street, New York,
NY 10016

2605

SMITHMARK books are available for bulk purchase for sales
promotion and premium use. For details write or call the
manager of special sales, SMITHMARK Publishers, Inc.
16 East 32nd Street, New York,
NY 10016; (212) 532-6600

Produced by CLB Publishing
Godalming Business Centre
Woolsack Way, Godalming, Surrey, UK

ISBN 0-7651-9342-6

Printed in China
10 9 8 7 6 5 4 3 2 1

Brigadier General Samuel Crawford of the Union army, seated here with members of his staff in 1862. Crawford was one of the officers at Fort Sumter when it fell to Confederate bombardment in April 1861.

Contents

1 War Is Coming!

Few people expected war. Abraham Lincoln, the United States' newly elected president, promised the nation, "There is no crisis. . . . There is nothing going wrong. . . . There shall be no bloodshed."

The year was 1861. Lincoln would go on to become one of the nation's greatest presidents—perhaps *the* greatest—but his predictions about the current crisis couldn't have been more wrong.

A horrible war was about to begin, a war that would pit North against South, brother against brother, father against son. Once begun, the Civil War—or, as some called it, the Brothers' War—would drag on for four long, miserable years.

It was the bloodiest struggle the young nation had ever experienced. More than 3 million Americans went to battle in this war; more than 600,000 died. During just two days of some Civil

John Brown (1800–1859) was a fiery abolitionist leader. He believed that slavery could only be abolished with force.

▼ Thanks to the free work of thousands of slaves, many Southern farmers ruled large plantations. These rich farmers lived in splendor in houses like this one in Natchez, Mississippi.

Slaves were forced to work in the fields from sunup to sundown. If there was a full moon, they worked longer.

◄ *Kansas was a new territory. Would it be a slave state or a free one? In 1854, Congress decided to let the people of Kansas decide for themselves. Terrible violence followed.*

▲ *In 1859, John Brown tried to start a slave rebellion. He and his small band of men took over this government building in Harpers Ferry, Virginia. Here, U.S. Marines storm the building.*

War battles, more American soldiers were killed than in *all* of the country's earlier wars.

IT CAN'T HAPPEN HERE: Though war seemed unthinkable to many, it had been coming for many years. And the issue that divided North and South, more than any other, was slavery.

Dutch slave traders had sold the first African slaves to English colonists in Jamestown, Virginia, in 1619. Back then, the settlers were struggling to start a new life in a new land. There was a huge amount of work to be done. The temptation to "buy" people, who would then work for free, proved irresistible.

Hundreds of thousands of slaves were soon kidnapped in Africa and sold to the states. Most were sold to farmers in the South, where they worked around the clock, helping grow tobacco.

The Northern states relied more on industry and manufacturing than on agriculture, and they soon outlawed slavery within their borders. But for Southern farmers, slaves had become crucial.

By the late 1700s, so much tobacco had been grown in the South that the soil was worn out. Throughout the nation, many now believed that the practice of slavery would die along with the tobacco industry.

It might have, except for the brainstorm of a Northerner named Eli Whitney (1765–1825). In 1792, Whitney visited a plantation in Savannah, Georgia. The planters told Whitney that they could easily grow lots of cotton, for a high profit, but it took slaves too long to separate cotton lint from cotton seed.

Whitney quickly designed a machine—the cotton gin—to help with the job. And the South's cotton industry was born.

By 1850, the South was exporting more than a million tons of cotton a year. And the number of slaves—men, women, and children—had risen to over 4 million. Most of these slaves worked in the fields helping to raise what planters now called King Cotton.

Meanwhile, in the North, the abolitionist movement—a movement to abolish slavery—was growing stronger every day. An escaped slave

▼ *The debate over Kansas's future was a fiery one. It would not be settled with speeches.*

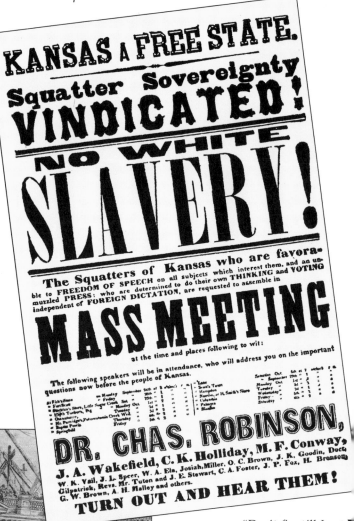

"*Don't fire till I get out of office," says President James Buchanan in this cartoon. He left the crisis to Lincoln.*

◄ *By the time Abraham Lincoln was sworn in as president on March 4, 1861, seven Southern states had already seceded— dropped out of the Union.*

▲ *White overseers, on horseback, watch as slaves pick cotton on a Mississippi plantation.*

▼ *Abolitionists spread the word on the evils of slavery. Fliers such as this showed slave children torn away from their mothers, and slaves whipped and hung.*

EMANCIPATOR—*EXTRA.*

NEW-YORK, SEPTEMBER 2, 1839.

American Anti-Slavery Almanac for 1840.

The seven cuts following, are selected from thirteen, which may be found in the Anti-Slavery Almanac for 1840. They represent well-authenticated facts, and illustrate in various ways, the cruelties daily inflicted upon three millions of native born Americans, by their fellow-countrymen! A brief explanation follows each cut.

The peculiar " Domestic Institutions of our Southern brethren."

Selling a Mother from her Child.

Mothers with young Children at work in the field.

named Frederick Douglass (1817–95) traveled from town to town, speaking out against the horrors of "owning" another human being. The self-taught Douglass spoke so powerfully that many refused to believe he had ever been a slave. But his message spread.

BLEEDING KANSAS: The young nation was growing, adding new states and territories. Should these states be slave states or free states? Northern and Southern states disagreed. In 1854, Congress passed the Kansas-Nebraska Act. The act declared that the people in these two new territories would have to decide the slavery issue for themselves.

They didn't settle the issue peacefully. Both sides organized and brought in weapons. So many settlers were shot, stabbed, and killed that Kansas became known as Bleeding Kansas.

Violence was spreading throughout the land—even to the halls of Congress. After one Northern senator spoke out against slavery, a Southern senator brutally beat him with his cane. War was closer than ever.

The First Shots

On Sunday night, October 16, 1859, 19 men rode into Harpers Ferry, Virginia. The group's leader was a tall, thin man named John Brown. Brown was an abolitionist. His plan was to give weapons to slaves and start a rebellion that would sweep across the South.

It didn't work out that way. Instead, Brown ended up taking hostages and holing up in an enginehouse. U.S. Marines, led by Lieutenant Colonel Robert E. Lee (1807–70), stormed the house. Brown was caught, tried for treason, and hung.

To the South, Brown was a villain, but many Northerners proclaimed Brown a hero. The hatred between South and North rose to a new pitch. Then, in 1860, the Republicans nominated for president an Illinois congressman who opposed slavery: Abraham Lincoln (1809–65).

Lincoln didn't advocate abolishing slavery altogether. He only opposed adding any new slave states or territories. Nevertheless, South Carolina made an extraordinary pledge. If Lincoln was elected president, the slave state vowed it would secede—drop out of the Union.

Lincoln did win, and South Carolina immediately made good on its pledge. It seceded. Six other Southern states followed suit. These states declared a new government for themselves—the Confederacy (an alliance, or

Captain Abner Doubleday was one of only 68 Union soldiers who were trapped in Fort Sumter for months.

The fort was in Charleston harbor. On shore were 6,000 South Carolina rebels. There was no way to get food and other supplies. Still, Major Robert Anderson, the Union officer in charge, refused to surrender.

On April 12, Confederate messengers rowed out to the fort. If Major Anderson didn't surrender by 4:00 A.M., they would open fire.

Anderson was from Kentucky—and a former slave owner. But he still refused.

▼ *Union soldiers held out for a day
and a half before surrendering.
Even though 3,341 shells hit the*

*tiny island, no one was killed.
But the fort itself sustained
heavy damage.*

league). On February 10, 1861, Mississippi
Senator Jefferson Davis (1808–89) was appointed
this new nation's first president.

When Lincoln was sworn into office on March
4, 1861, there were rumors that rebels would
assassinate him. Lincoln had to slip into
Washington at night, in disguise. But he kept
begging the Southern states to rejoin the Union.

Then came the attack on Fort Sumter. For
months, the Confederacy had been taking over
government buildings, without a fight. But the
Union soldiers at Fort Sumter, on an island in
South Carolina's harbor, refused to surrender.
The Confederates vowed to attack.

On April 12, at 4:30 A.M., General Pierre
Beauregard gave the order to his Confederate
soldiers to fire on Fort Sumter. War had begun.

To War! The Rush to Enlist

At the time of the attack on Fort Sumter, the Union army had only 17,000 soldiers. And most of these men were stationed in the west. President Lincoln immediately sent out a call urging Northern men to volunteer, and thousands of Northerners rushed to join his army.

The trouble was, Lincoln's call to enlist was also heard in the South, and the newly formed Confederacy hastened to defend itself. So many men tried to join the rebel army, in fact, that hundreds had to be turned away.

At the time, the soldier with the best reputation in the land was a Virginia officer named Robert E. Lee. Lee had been a hero in the Mexican War (1846–48) and had led the capture of John Brown at Harpers Ferry. He was said to be a superb commander. Lincoln promptly asked Lee to head the Union army.

For Lee, the decision was hard. His own state was considering joining the Confederacy. How could he lead the fight against his own people? Then, five days after the fall of Fort Sumter, Virginia voted to secede. Lee announced he would command Virginia's army, not Lincoln's.

WILL WASHINGTON FALL?: What if the Southern troops attacked Washington? Would the nation's capital fall?

The possibility was real. Lincoln's volunteers had yet to arrive. The White House was guarded only by a small band of civilian volunteers, led by Senator James H. Lane and aging General-in-Chief Winfield Scott. Scott was a war hero. Lane had lived through the fighting in Bleeding Kansas, so he, too, had some combat experience. But with thousands of rebel troops just south of Washington in Virginia, how long could Lane and Scott be expected to hold off an all-out attack?

General Scott drew up an emergency plan. In case of attack, Lincoln and his advisers would barricade themselves in the basement of the thick-walled Treasury building and try to last on water and 2,000 barrels of flour.

Where were the troops? Aides saw Lincoln pacing back and forth in his office. "Why don't they come?" worried Lincoln. "Why don't they come?

▲ At first, the Union accepted no black soldiers into its army. But the navy was a different story, as here, on the Mendota.

▼ When the war began, soldiers on both sides were totally untrained. By the time of this battle, at Cedar Creek in 1864, the soldiers on both sides had been hardened by endless fighting.

At last, on April 25, the Northern troops arrived, and the soldiers quickly went to work setting up camps and forts. By the time they were done, 74 forts circled the capital city. Washington was safe—for now.

◀ *Rebel troops relax in their camp. Before the war began, both sides expected an easy victory.*

▲ *The 67th New York Infantry trains at Camp Proctor. For both sides, providing so many men with uniforms, equipment, and weapons was a tremendous feat of organization.*

Massachusetts soldiers man the ▶ cannon at Fort Totten, north of Washington. The capital now had more protection than any other city in the world.

At the time, no one could have ▶ predicted the massive battles that would follow. Here, at Resaca, thousands of Union infantry, artillerymen, and cavalry clash with the Army of Tennessee.

The President Grows Impatient

The rebels had set up their new government in Richmond, Virginia, not far at all from the Union's capital in Washington. Now that Lincoln had his own capital defended, would he send troops to storm the capital of the Confederacy?

The rebel army thought so. General Beauregard, who had led the battle at Fort Sumter, expected the Union attack at any moment. Beauregard began moving his 35,000 Confederate soldiers northward, preparing to stop the Union charge.

But the charge did not come. The Union commander, Irvin McDowell, thought his new

▲ On April 19, only one week after the attack on Fort Sumter, Lincoln declared a blockade of the rebel coast.

◄ Good roads—roads that could take heavy use—were vital for supplying armies. They were also rare. Here, Union engineers built a bridge using logs covered with soil and gravel.

▼ Railroads would prove essential to the war effort, as another way of moving troops, weapons, ammo, and food. This is the base camp of the Union's Railroad Construction Corps at City Point, Virginia, under General George McClellan's command.

recruits weren't yet ready for the rigors of battle. "This is not an army," he told President Lincoln flatly. He wanted more time to train, time to mold his men into soldiers.

But Lincoln was growing impatient. He had asked his soldiers to enlist for a term of three months. The time was almost up. Lincoln also pointed out to his general that the Confederate army was as undertrained as the Union forces. The time to strike, he said, was now.

The Union troops finally started to move south on July 18. The volunteers—37,000 of them—marched out of Maryland and into Virginia. The new soldiers were unruly. As General McDowell reported, "They stopped every moment to pick blackberries or get water. They would not keep their ranks, order as much as you pleased. . . ."

A crowd had come out from Washington to watch. The spectators, who included a number of senators, brought picnic baskets. They thought the Union would destroy the rebels in one quick strike, and figured the battle would be fun to watch—a game between the blue-uniformed Union and the Confederate gray.

What the Union didn't know was, Beauregard was waiting for them.

2 The Long Beginning

Maryland was a Southern state, with slave owners. Many of its citizens were sympathetic to the rebel cause. One of these rebel sympathizers was a Mrs. Rose O'Neal Greenhow, a rich Washington woman. When Lincoln's troops marched out of the capital, she sent a warning to General Beauregard, writing the message in code and hiding it in the hair of a young Southern girl.

Alerted to the coming attack, Beauregard had his men form an eight-mile line on the other side of a creek known as Bull Run. There they waited.

It took McDowell's men four days to reach the creek. The blue-clad men started moving across it at nine on a Sunday morning, July 21, 1861.

They were greeted by a whir of bullets. But they kept marching forward.

As the first wounded men were carried back, other soldiers, seeing the terrors of war for the first time, vomited in horror.

But the Union blue kept up the attack. And it started to work. By noon, the Union had overrun the whole left side of the gray line. The Confederate

◄ *President James Buchanan was still in power when the states seceded. He opposed the secession but failed to act. He left the problem to his successor.*

▲ *Born in a log cabin, the son of a poor farmer, Lincoln was self-taught. This portrait, one of the most famous, was taken in 1864 and appears on the $5 bill.*

14

Losing Lee to the Confederacy would prove a horrible blow to the Union cause, and Lincoln would go through many generals before he found an able commander. Here, he confers with General McClellan at Antietam. McClellan's caution cost the lives of thousands.

◄ *Andrew Johnson was a Southern Democrat and slave owner, but he believed secession was wrong. He stayed loyal to the Union and became vice president-elect in 1864.*

▲ *Jefferson Davis, the Confederacy's first and only president, was a devout believer in slavery. A former war hero, Davis had twice served as a Mississippi senator.*

troops were running. General McDowell, on his horse, waved a white-gloved hand as he announced to his troops that they had won a great victory. The Northerners cheered wildly. So did the spectators from Washington, who were watching from the safety of a nearby hill.

THE GREAT SKEDADDLE: They cheered too soon. Standing on top of a hill in the middle of the Southern line was a group of Virginia soldiers led by Thomas J. Jackson. As the Confederates ran, a Southern general rallied his men by pointing to Jackson, who was "standing like a stone wall." It was a nickname that would stick, and Stonewall Jackson (1824–63) would come to be a name the Union feared.

The courage of Jackson's men spread to the rest of the troops. The Union attack was stopped. And rebel reserves began to arrive. Beauregard commanded his whole army to charge, and Jackson cried to his men, "Yell like furies!" As the men charged, they howled what would come to be known as the rebel yell.

It was the Union troops who now turned and ran. So did the spectators. Later, it would be called the Great Skedaddle, but at the time, it was no joke. Soldiers and onlookers rushed pell-mell through Bull Run stream; many drowned.

The first major battle of the war had been fought, and the Union had suffered a humiliating defeat. Many on both sides thought the war was now over.

Hurry Up and Wait

Promising that he would not give up until he had brought the Union back together, President Lincoln called for more volunteers, men who were willing to serve longer than three months each. Then he appointed a new general-in-chief. He also ordered more ships to join his blockade of the Southern ports.

The goal of the blockade was to keep the South from shipping cotton to England and from bringing other goods back in, thus crippling the Confederacy's economy.

LITTLE MAC: The general Lincoln now chose was barrel-chested George McClellan (1826–85), affectionately known to his soldiers as Little Mac. McClellan was a powerful man who could bend coins with his bare hands. He was also a war hero who had finished second in his class at West Point. He seemed—to Lincoln, to his men, and to his country—like an excellent choice to lead the Army of the Potomac.

McClellan spent the rest of the summer and fall drilling his troops. Lincoln urged him to move, but McClellan refused. He said that 150,000 rebels waited for him just outside Washington, and asked for more men. The rebels had great cannons, he said. Most federal spies said that the Union army outnumbered its enemy three to one. But McClellan continued to believe what he wanted to believe.

Then, in September 1861, the rebel troops near Washington retreated. The great cannons that had scared McClellan turned out to be fakes, big logs set up to decoy the cautious general.

McClellan was still not convinced that he

▲ When Lincoln was elected, his general-in-chief was Winfield Scott. At 75, Scott was still fiery and crafty, but he was now too heavy to ride a horse and far too old for battle.

◀ Powerful George McClellan seemed like the perfect choice for Union general-in-chief. But his tremendous cautiousness in battle badly hurt the North.

General Ulysses Simpson ▶ Grant, fifth from the right, in 1864, with his staff. On March 9 of that year, Lincoln had made him his ninth general-in-chief.

should begin his march. Winter came. McClellan had not moved. Terribly frustrated, Lincoln gave McClellan an ultimatum. He must begin the war by February 22, 1862, Washington's birthday.

Lincoln wanted the army to march back to Bull Run, then on to Richmond. McClellan said this was much too dangerous. He had his own plan. He would surprise Lee's troops by traveling down the Chesapeake Bay and attacking from the east.

He finally started to move his men on February 27. There was just one little problem. The boats he had built to carry his army (at a cost of $1 million) wouldn't fit through the canal!

VICTORIES IN THE WEST: Not all the news was bad. In the west, Union armies had captured two forts, which would help them control key Southern rivers, the Tennessee and the Cumberland. The general who had won these battles was Ulysses S. Grant (1822–85). Grant was unknown to the country at the time. That would quickly change.

▲ *Known for his violent temper, rebel General Braxton Bragg was hated by his troops. But he had a staunch ally in Confederate President Jefferson Davis.*

▼ *Without General Robert Edward Lee, the South probably would have lost quickly. Again and again, his brilliant battle plans guided the outnumbered Confederacy to victory.*

17

The Monitor *vs. the* Merrimack

New wars often lead to new weapons, and the Civil War was no exception. In fact, this war began a total revolution in navy warfare.

At the start of the war, the Confederacy had no navy, no ships to defend against the Yankee blockade. But they were working feverishly on a special weapon they hoped would turn the tide of the sea battle—a ship with iron sides. She was actually a wooden Union ship, captured by the South, with sheets of metal bolted onto the sides.

News of the South's plans terrified the Union leaders. To defend himself against this new threat, Lincoln turned to John Ericsson (1803–89), a Swedish immigrant and inventor. Ericsson hastily designed his own ironclad, the *Monitor*.

A SINKING FEELING: Ericsson's design called for a revolving turret of guns on top of a ship made completely out of iron. He promised that his ship would take to the water like a duck, but Lincoln's naval advisers were doubtful. A ship made *entirely* of iron? Surely it would sink. But Lincoln overruled his advisers and the ship was built.

The *Monitor* began her maiden voyage on January 30, 1862. Everything that could go

▲ *Union General Winfield Scott Hancock (1824–86), who bravely rallied his troops at Gettysburg and in other critical battles. McClellan called him Hancock the Superb.*

▼ *General Ambrose Burnside, seated, arms folded, with his staff. He accepted command of the federal troops reluctantly.*

◀ *William Tecumseh Sherman, the thin, red-haired general from Ohio. After early Union defeats, Sherman went home to his wife. According to McClellan, he was "gone in the head" and, indeed, was thinking of killing himself. But Grant brought him back, and he went on to lead the devastating attack known as Sherman's March.*

After a distinguished naval career, ▶
Rear Admiral D. G. Farragut proved
a fearless leader in the Union's
Mississippi campaign. Afraid of
heights, he had his men tie him
to the mast. As his fleet sailed
through treacherous mines
(then known as torpedoes), he
shouted, "Damn the torpedoes,
full steam ahead!"

The bravery of Union General ▶
George "Pap" Thomas (1816–70)
once saved the Union army
from a rout and earned
him the nickname
Rock of Chickamauga.

◀ *General G. G. Meade was*
abruptly given command of
the Army of the Potomac on
June 18, 1863. He forced
battle on General Lee's
Confederate armies before
Gettysburg—a turning point
of the war.

wrong, did. First, the ship's rudder didn't work,
and the boat careened back and forth across
Manhattan's East River. At sea, the boat leaked.
Gas fumes knocked the men unconscious. Still,
the strange boat struggled southward.

THE *MERRIMACK* ATTACK: On March 8, the
South's *Merrimack* was ready for battle. The
ironclad sailed right up to the Union navy. The
Union men had never seen a ship like this one.
They fired at her, but their cannonballs bounced
harmlessly off the enemy's iron hide. The
Merrimack had soon destroyed three Union ships.
She was battering a fourth ship, the *Minnesota,*
when darkness fell.

The crew of the *Minnesota* did not go to sleep
that night. They knew that the morning would
bring their death.

And then, in the middle of the night, the
Monitor finally sailed toward them.

The next morning, the *Merrimack* was met by
one of her own kind. For four and a half hours,
the two strange ships banged together, firing
away at each other with everything they had.
Neither ship was seriously damaged. The fight
was a draw. Lincoln's navy was saved.

Little Mac's "Victory"

On March 17, 1862, McClellan's great sneak attack got under way at last. It took 400 boats to float the Army of the Potomac (121,500 soldiers, 14,592 horses and mules) all the way to Fortress Monroe on the coast of Virginia.

The plan was to march east to Richmond, storm the capital of the new upstart government, and end the war. That was the plan. But then McClellan arrived at Yorktown.

Stationed at Yorktown was rebel commander John Bankhead Magruder with only 11,000 men. If McClellan attacked, Magruder would be forced to surrender or face slaughter.

Trying to stave off disaster, Magruder put on a show. He ordered one battalion to march through a clearing in a circle. From a distance, McClellan couldn't tell that he was seeing the same men over and over again. It seemed like an incredible parade of soldiers. McClellan sent a telegraph message to Washington. He was up against the entire Confederate army. He needed more men.

Lincoln wired back immediately, ordering McClellan to strike at once. McClellan ignored the order. He had his men pass the time digging trenches. He also used one of the Union's newest weapons: an observation balloon designed by inventor Thaddeus Lowe (1832–1913).

▼ *Tough reb General James Longstreet (1821–1904). Old Pete from Georgia was equally admired by his men and by his commanding officer, Robert E. Lee.*

Daring Southern cavalry ▶ leader Jubal Anderson Early (1816–94). He and his men held the entire town of Chambersburg, Pennsylvania, hostage for $500,000. When the town didn't pay, Early set the city ablaze.

▼ *Stonewall Jackson would earn his nickname many times over. In 1862, he waged a remarkable campaign against the Union in the Shenandoah Valley.*

▲ In the moment of victory, Stonewall Jackson is accidentally shot by his own men. The wound proved fatal.

Lowe himself would float up in the hydrogen balloon to get a better look at the enemy. The balloon was kept carefully anchored to the ground, but on one trip, with General Fitz-John Porter aboard, the balloon broke free in the wind and sent Porter sailing toward the enemy. He was able to land the balloon in time.

McClellan, meanwhile, used hundreds of horses to drag huge guns into position. The one thing he did not do was attack.

And his delay allowed thousands of rebels under General Joseph E. Johnston to ride down from Richmond. Magruder's trick had worked.

READY OR NOT: A month passed. Finally, on the night before McClellan decided he was ready to begin his attack, the Confederates stunned him with an all-out aerial bombardment. Fires burst out everywhere as rebel artillery boomed. Shells arced into McClellan's camp.

The next morning, the federal troops discovered the reason for the fireworks. The Confederates had used the bombardment to hide their retreat. Thanks once again to McClellan's delay, the rebel army had escaped. Only Little Mac declared Yorktown a victory.

3 A Seething Hell

The poet Walt Whitman, who volunteered in Union hospitals, called the war "a seething hell."

Whitman saw thousands of wounded men. He saw doctors sawing off limb after limb, without painkillers, as they tried to save the dying soldiers.

With medical science still in its infancy, more men were dying of scurvy, pneumonia, and other diseases than were dying in battle.

But if Whitman had seen the battles themselves, he would have seen an even worse nightmare. The Brothers' War had now begun in deadly earnest, and fellow countrymen were butchering each other by the thousands.

THE BLOODIEST BATTLE: While McClellan stalled at Yorktown, Grant and 42,000 troops camped in Tennessee. They were waiting for the Army of the Ohio, under General Don Carlos Buell (1818–98). The plan was for the two armies to join together and then attack the Confederate army under General Albert Sidney Johnston (1803–62) in Mississippi.

But General Johnston had a different plan. On April 6, 1862, Johnston's men launched a fierce, surprise attack.

The rebel attack almost caused a Union massacre. But the Union troops were saved by a band of soldiers under

▲ The war's terrible demand for soldiers brought opportunities for young officers, such as these of the Union. On both sides, many young commanders would reach the rank of general.

◄ Union mounted and foot officers confer.

▼ This 1863 West Point class could almost pass as modern. The war proved West Point's quality—it had trained the leading officers of both sides.

General Benjamin Prentiss. These men were cornered in a part of the woods that came to be known as the Hornet's Nest. Though the Union troops were surrounded by the enemy on three sides, they managed to hold on for almost six hours. Those six hours allowed the rest of the Union army to retreat and regroup.

COUNTING THE DEAD: It was two days before the armies pulled out. Many men stayed behind, lying all over the field of battle. In just two days of fighting, more than 20,000 men had been wounded and 3,477 men had died.

The ferocious battle was named Shiloh, after the small white church where much fighting occurred. Shiloh in Hebrew means "place of peace." But for the country, Shiloh would now have a different meaning. If there was anyone left who thought the war could be ended quickly, without much bloodshed, they could no longer believe it now.

◄ *The triumphant cavalry officer Jeb Stuart. Above him, portraits of Jackson, Lee, and Johnston are flanked by the first Confederate army flags.*

▼ *Confederate troops camped at Warrington Navy Yard, Pensacola, Florida. Throughout the war, the South lacked money. Uniforms were often scarce.*

▼ *Colonel Micah Jenkins, Palmetto Sharpshooters Regiment. Like many other top rebel officers, Jenkins had been a U.S. Army regular before the war.*

The War Seesaws

At the same time as the disaster of Shiloh, the North scored a major victory. Sixty-year-old Admiral David G. Farragut (1801–70) led a Union fleet up the Mississippi. His assignment was to take New Orleans, a key port.

If the North could control the Mississippi River, it would deliver a crippling blow to the South, cutting it in two and taking away a vital means of transportation.

But the task seemed impossible. To get to New Orleans, Farragut would have to sail past Forts Jackson and St. Philip. The Confederates had filled the river around the forts with old boats. These obstacles were there to stall Farragut's fleet while the forts' cannons sunk him.

Farragut decided he had no choice. Under cover of darkness, he attempted to sail past the forts. Then the moon came out, and the cannons began blasting, smashing shots into the ships. His fleet was on fire. But somehow Farragut and his crews managed to get past.

Four ships were lost. But enough of the fleet survived to capture New Orleans.

▼ By a wrecked log cabin, a soldier cares for one of his wounded fellows.

▼ An actor in the film Glory portrays a first sergeant of the 54th Massachusetts Regiment, the first black regiment. The bravery of these troops soon made them famous.

◄ The war effort got into gear quickly. Here, early in the war, Michigan privates already have standard uniforms and weapons.

▲ In 1863, Lincoln started a draft but allowed men to pay for substitutes. In protest, poor men in New York, who couldn't afford to pay their way out, rioted for four days.

Though his uniform is gray, this is a Union soldier, part of the famous Seventh New York State Militia, which was formed from ◄ the states' top families.

▼ When this picture was taken, these Wisconsin volunteers had already seen fierce fighting in battles such as Vicksburg.

STONEWALL THE WIZARD: All this time, McClellan moved slowly toward Richmond, constantly demanding more troops from Washington. There were three federal armies nearby, in the Shenandoah Valley. McClellan wanted them to join him, but they were all busy with one man—Stonewall Jackson.

Leading just 17,000 men, always greatly outnumbered, Jackson kept studying his huge 8½-foot-long map of the valley as he planned his next surprise attack or daring escape. From April to May of 1862, his tiny army made off with huge quantities of supplies, supplies that the South desperately needed.

MCCLELLAN'S FINAL SEVEN DAYS: Until now, McClellan's foe had been Gen. J. E. Johnston. When Johnston was wounded, President Davis assigned Robert E. Lee to take over.

For seven straight days, the two armies clashed, with Lee outsmarting McClellan every time. McClellan kept retreating, ignoring his aides as they pleaded with him to counterattack. Little Mac was driven far back from Richmond.

Antietam

Lincoln had had enough, and he fired McClellan. But his replacement, John Pope (1822–92), didn't fare much better.

First, Stonewall Jackson's men, outnumbered as always, somehow managed to fight Pope's army to a standoff. Next, Jeb Stuart's cavalry raided Pope's headquarters and got away with $35,000 and a detailed guide to the Union positions. Then, Stonewall Jackson marched his men right around Pope's army, cutting off Pope's supply line back to Washington.

When Pope finally caught up with Jackson, the Southern commander was waiting for him on the same hill he had held in the first battle of Bull Run.

The second Bull Run made the first battle seem like a mild argument. This time, 25,000 men were killed or wounded.

LITTLE MAC'S BACK: Lincoln needed Pope in the west. That left him with no choice but to put McClellan back in charge of the Army of the Potomac.

McClellan led his army after Lee's, but as usual, the cautious general didn't catch up with his foe.

▲ *A Civil War pistol, with two triggers. One trigger turned the six-shot chamber; the other trigger fired the gun.*

▼ *The Fourth U.S. Colored Infantry. Northern blacks were eager to fight for their race's freedom. But the North didn't allow blacks to enlist until 1863.*

Once they had a chance, ▶ *blacks enlisted in droves. They quickly proved to be some of the most heroic soldiers in the war.*

▼ *Colonel Hiram Berdan, First U.S. Sharpshooters—his regiment was famous for its shooting skills. Their rifles carried telescopic sights.*

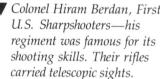

As his army moved through a camp that Lee had abandoned, one of McClellan's corporals picked up three cigars. The cigars were wrapped in paper. On the paper were Lee's orders to his small army, which he had split into two forces.

Half of the army had gone on a mission led by Stonewall Jackson, while Lee led the other half in an attack on a federal railway center. The Confederate army, outmanned to begin with, was now doubly vulnerable. And McClellan had the proof right in his hand.

He wired Lincoln with the good news, promising an immediate defeat of Robert E. Lee. But one more agonizing time, McClellan waited.

Across the tiny creek known as Antietam was Lee's army of a mere 18,000. McClellan had 95,000 men. But he remained convinced that he faced a much larger force, and for two crucial days, he planned and prepared.

What would have happened if he had attacked? Many say it would have ended the war, then and there. By waiting, McClellan gave time for Jackson's men to rush back to rejoin Lee. Instead of crushing Lee, McClellan now faced the bloodiest day of fighting in the entire war.

More than 22,000 men were wounded or killed. More Northerners were hurt than were Southerners. But Lee's army was smaller to begin with. He couldn't afford the losses.

Thanks to reinforcements, McClellan now had Lee cornered and outnumbered. But one last time, he waited. Lincoln would wait no more.

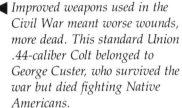

◀ Improved weapons used in the Civil War meant worse wounds, more dead. This standard Union .44-caliber Colt belonged to George Custer, who survived the war but died fighting Native Americans.

▼ Wounds inflicted by these Civil War muskets were much worse than those from a modern rifle. When the soft lead bullets hit a limb, the bone splintered badly.

This .36-caliber Colt ▶ pistol was the cavalry's favored handgun. It proved effective, though there was so much close fighting, it was often used as a club!

◀ Union troops rest after a drill session near Petersburg, Virginia. Nearby are the men's Enfield-type muskets, stacked in tripods, ready for use.

Freeing the Slaves

After the bloody carnage at Antietam, Lincoln fired McClellan for the second and last time.

The next week, the president made an even more momentous decision: He issued the Emancipation Proclamation. His proclamation stated that all slaves held in the Confederacy were to be set free.

Until then, the war had been officially fought only to preserve the Union. According to stated policy, if the Southern states ended their policy of secession, they could still keep their slaves.

With the proclamation, all that changed, and the North had a new reason to fight—a moral reason. It had become a war to free the slaves.

Abolitionists and blacks everywhere celebrated Lincoln's announcement. But freeing the slaves was easier said than done. First, the North would have to win. At the moment, that seemed like a very hard task.

"MURDER, NOT WARFARE": McClellan's replacement was General Ambrose E. Burnside (1824–81), the man whose huge muttonchop whiskers came to be known as sideburns. Eager to show he wasn't overly cautious like McClellan, Burnside quickly proved himself to be much too rash.

He caught up with Lee at Fredericksburg, where Lee's smaller army was dug in and well positioned. On a hill known as Marye's Heights, the Confederate army massed behind a stone

▲ *Union heavy battery, Fort Brady on the James. Note the wheel in the foreground, which allowed the men to swivel the massive cannon.*

▼ *Captain John C. Tidball (right) and his staff of Battery A, Second U.S. Artillery. In each battery, one captain oversaw six guns.*

▲ *The Connecticut heavy artillery at Fort Richardson. The cannonballs fired in a straight line and were lethal for many yards after first grazing the ground.*

The barrel of this cannon weighed 12,500 pounds. It was made by pouring layers of metal around a core, as opposed to casting a solid piece of metal and boring out the hole.

◀ *Inventor Thaddeus Lowe designed a portable apparatus for inflating his observation balloon, the* Intrepid. *Here, the balloon is inflated for the battle of Fair Oaks, 1862.*

▲ *A modern-day reenactment of the mortar battles waged in the Civil War. Mortars were short cannons used for lobbing shot at high angles, up and over enemy fortifications.*

wall, overlooking a long field. Behind the rebel infantry, a row of cannons pointed down the hill. General Lee was sure that Burnside would not attack the heights.

But Burnside ordered the bulk of his army to charge up Marye's Heights. His aides tried to talk him out of it. One said that such a charge would be "murder, not warfare." Burnside held firm.

He sent his men up the hill 14 times. Row after row of blue-coated Union soldiers marched into the roaring cannon fire and the rush of bullets.

When Burnside at last gave up, the Confederates had mowed down 9,000 of his men.

ANOTHER GENERAL, ANOTHER DEFEAT: Again Lincoln replaced his general-in-chief, this time with General Joe Hooker (1814–79). But the North's woes continued.

January 1, 1863, marked the beginning of the third year of the war, the war the North had hoped to end so quickly. And after a long, bleak winter, the new year began with yet another Union defeat.

Once again, Lee was outnumbered, this time two to one. Once again, he managed to outsmart the North. This time, the battle came at Chancellorsville. . . .

Lee Splits in Two

Hooker had a new plan for capturing and destroying Lee and his army, a plan that Hooker believed was surefire.

"My plans are perfect," announced the general immodestly. "May God have mercy on General Lee, for *I* will have none."

His enthusiasm spread to the troops. Soon everyone was repeating the same phrase: "Lee is in our power!"

President Lincoln wanted to believe that Hooker and his men were right, but he also cautioned them not to boast too soon.

Hooker planned to split his mighty army in two. He would leave one group at Fredericksburg, facing Lee's forces. These men would attack hard enough to keep Lee occupied. In the meantime, Hooker would sneak most of his troops around to the north, march along the river, then swing around and come back at Lee's men from behind, thus surrounding them in an all-out attack.

Lee's defense: Lee quickly figured out what was going on. But now he had to decide how to defend himself.

Hooker commanded 115,000 soldiers. Lee had only 60,000. Could he afford to become any smaller?

Standard military strategy said no, and it never occurred to Hooker that Lee would even consider such a plan. But now Lee split his army in two, just as Hooker had done, and half of his men rushed back to defend against Hooker's attack.

Hooker's men were coming through the woods near Chancellorsville when the rebels opened fire. Stunned, Hooker ordered a rapid retreat.

Bolder plans: The first day of fighting had been a tremendous Southern success. At midnight, Lee met with Stonewall Jackson, his most valued general. Jackson now had an even bolder plan—to split Lee's army in half yet again!

The next day, having convinced his commander to approve his maneuver, Jackson led his men around Hooker's right flank. To get there, they used a local townsperson to guide them through the thick, dark woods. When they emerged, the rebels again surprised Hooker.

Following up the success of ▶ the Monitor *were ironclads like this one, the* St. Louis, *a steamboat with armored sides.*

◀ *A second lieutenant of the U.S. Marines strikes a favorite pose of the period. He wears a double-breasted, dark blue frock coat and kepi (hat), and light blue trousers with thin, red stripes.*

▼ *The U.S. Navy crew of the* Mendota, *on the James. As the war effort staggered the South's economy, the North's naval blockade tightened its stranglehold.*

A Union survivor remembers the surprise attack as a sudden "whirlwind of men." Jackson drove the Union army backward all day.

LEE'S RIGHT ARM: That night, Jackson was eager to press his advantage and was even considering continuing the battle in darkness. He rode out past his own lines to study the enemy forces and drew gunfire. He quickly rode back, but now some of his own men panicked and opened fire. He was hit three times in his left arm, and the arm had to be amputated.

"He has lost his left arm," mourned Lee, "but I have lost my right."

Lee had lost him for good. A high fever soon set in, and on Sunday, May 10, 1863, Stonewall Jackson died, calling out feverish orders to his troops till the last second.

The South had lost one of its greatest heroes. But the North was suffering another massive defeat. As the Confederates fired after the fleeing Union army, their shots set fire to the dry woods, which were filled with Union wounded. Hooker's troops had to flee with the cries of their own men ringing in their ears, as the fire in the woods blazed on.

▲ *A full view of the* Mendota, *a boat with both sails and steam power*

Captain Winslow (left) *and* ▶ *officers of the* Kearsage, *the sloop that sank the rebels' best blockade-runner, the* Alabama

◀ *The men pose in front of the* Monitor's *battle-scarred turret. It was dented but never broken by the ironclad* Merrimack.

4 The Siege Continues

A map that showed *all* of the battle sites of the Civil War would have to be huge. North and South waged battle in 10,000 different places!

This map shows some of the key sites. The circled numbers on the map refer to the chronology of battles listed below. The map's solid black lines show the railroad routes.

Early Fighting
1 Boonville (June 17, 1861)
2 First Bull Run (Manassas) (July 21, 1861)
3 Wilson's Creek (August 10, 1861)
4 Cheat Mountain (September 11, 1861)
5 Ball's Bluff (October 21, 1861)
6 Belmont (November 7, 1861)
7 Kernstown (March 23, 1862)

Valley Campaign, Spring 1862
8 McDowell (May 8, 1862)
9 Front Royal (May 23, 1862)
10 First Winchester (May 25, 1862)
11 Cross Keys (June 8, 1862)
12 Port Republic (June 9, 1862)
13 Second Bull Run (August 29–30, 1862)
14 Chantilly (September 1, 1862)
15 South Mountain (September 14, 1862)
16 Antietam (September 17, 1862)

Peninsula Campaign, 1862
17 Seven Pines/Fair Oaks (May 31–June 1, 1862)
18 Mechanicsville (June 26, 1862)
19 Seven Days' Battle (June 25–July 1, 1862)
20 Malvern Hill (July 1, 1862)

Fredericksburg, 1862
21 Fredericksburg (December 13, 1862)

Western Campaigns, 1862—West of Mississippi
22 Pea Ridge (March 6–8, 1862)
23 Prairie Grove (December 7, 1862)

Western Campaigns, 1862—East of Mississippi
24 Mill Springs (January 19–20, 1862)
25 Fort Donelson (February 14–16, 1862)
26 Shiloh (April 6–7, 1862)
27 Richmond (August 30, 1862)
28 Iuka (September 19–20, 1862)
29 Corinth (October 2–4, 1862)
30 Perryville (October 8, 1862)
31 Stones River (December 31, 1862–January 2, 1863)

Mississippi River Campaign, 1862
32 Island No. 10 (April 7–8, 1862)
33 New Orleans (April 18–29, 1862)
34 Plum Run Bend (May 10, 1862)
35 Memphis (June 6, 1862)
36 Chickasaw Bayou, Vicksburg (December 29, 1862)

Big Black River Campaign, 1863
37 Jackson (May 14, 1863)

Tennessee River Campaign, 1863
38 Chickamauga (September 19–20, 1863)
39 Chattanooga (November 23–25, 1863)

Eastern Campaigns, 1863–64
40 Chancellorsville (May 1–4, 1863)
41 Beverly Ford and Brandy Station (June 9, 1863)
42 Second Winchester (June 13–15, 1863)
43 Gettysburg (July 1–3, 1863)
44 Culpeper (September 13, 1863)
45 Bristoe Station (October 14, 1863)
46 Mine Run (November 26–28, 1863)
47 Olustee (February 20, 1864)
48 Wilderness (May 5–7, 1864)
49 Spotsylvania (May 8–19, 1864)
50 Yellow Tavern (May 11, 1864)
51 Drewry's Bluff (May 12–16, 1864)
52 New Market (May 15, 1864)
53 North Anna River (May 23–28, 1864)
54 Hawes Shop (May 27–28, 1864)
55 Cold Harbor (June 1–12, 1864)

Valley Campaign, 1864–65
56 Monacacy River (July 9, 1864)
57 Kernstown (July 23–24, 1864)
58 Winchester/Kernstown (July 23–24, 1864)
59 Third Winchester (September 19–22, 1864)
60 Fisher's Hill (September 21–22, 1864)
61 Cedar Creek (October 19, 1864)
62 Waynesboro (March 2, 1865)

Red River Expedition, 1864
63 Sabine Crossroads (April 8–9, 1864)
64 Pleasant Hill (April 8–9, 1864)

Missouri Campaign, 1864
65 Lexington (September 18–October 16, 1864)
66 Independence (October 22, 1864)
67 Westport (October 23, 1864)

Mississippi Campaign, 1864
68 Okolona (February 22, 1864)
69 Brice's Crossroads (June 10, 1864)
70 Tupelo Expedition (July 5–18, 1864)

Atlanta Campaign, 1864–65
71 Kennesaw Mountain (June 9–27, 1864)
72 Peachtree Creek (July 20, 1864)
73 Siege of Atlanta (July–September 1864)
74 Ezra Church (July 28, 1864)
75 Jonesboro (August 31, 1864)
76 Franklin (November 30, 1864)
77 Nashville (December 2, 1864)
78 Bentonville (March 19–21, 1865)

Petersburg and Richmond Siege, 1864–65
79 Globe Tavern (August 18, 1864)
80 Hatcher's Run (February 5–7, 1865)
81 Dinwiddie Court House and White Oak Road (March 31, 1865)
82 Five Forks (April 1, 1865)

Concluding Actions
83 Sayler's Creek (April 6, 1865)
84 Appomattox Court House (April 8–9, 1865)

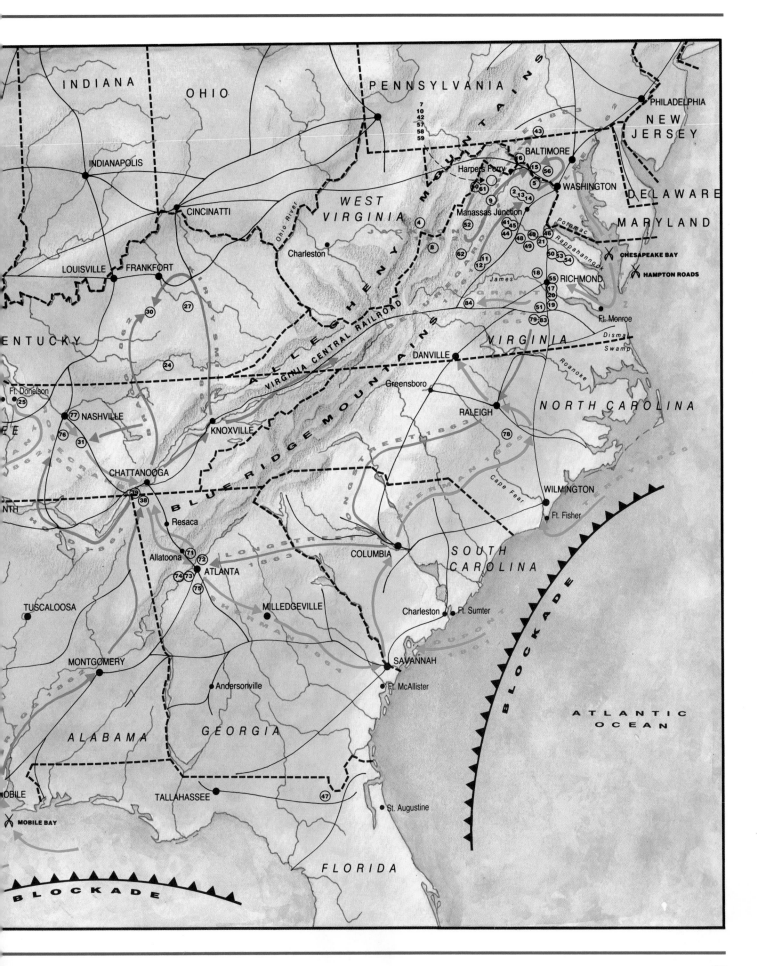

INDIANA

OHIO

PENNSYLVANIA

PHILADELPHIA

NEW JERSEY

7
10
42
57
58
59

43

INDIANAPOLIS

BALTIMORE

6
15 56
5
WASHINGTON

DELAWARE

Harpers Ferry

MARYLAND

WEST VIRGINIA

CINCINATTI

50 51
9
2 13 14

Manassas Junction

4

52

41 45
44

48 46
49 21

Poromac

CHESAPEAKE BAY

HAMPTON ROADS

Charleston

8

62

11

12

50 53 54

18 55

RICHMOND

Rappahannock

James

17
20
51 19

Ft. Monroe

79 83

LOUISVILLE

FRANKFORT

KENTUCKY

27

30

24

Ohio River

Virginia Central Railroad

VIRGINIA

Dismal Swamp

ALLEGHENY MOUNTAINS

DANVILLE

84

GRANT

Roanoke

Ft. Donelson

25

Greensboro

NORTH CAROLINA

NASHVILLE

77

76

KNOXVILLE

RALEIGH

78

31

BLUE RIDGE MOUNTAINS

CHATTANOOGA

39
38

Resaca

WILMINGTON

Ft. Fisher

Cape Fear

71
72

Allatoona

74 73
ATLANTA

75

COLUMBIA

SOUTH CAROLINA

TUSCALOOSA

MILLEDGEVILLE

Charleston
Ft. Sumter

MONTGOMERY

Andersonville

SAVANNAH

Ft. McAllister

BLOCKADE

ATLANTIC OCEAN

ALABAMA

GEORGIA

MOBILE

TALLAHASSEE

47

St. Augustine

MOBILE BAY

FLORIDA

BLOCKADE

Women at War

As the brutal war dragged on and on, the nation's men were not the only ones who were caught in the struggle. Wherever battles were fought, women were there as well, risking their lives to nurse the wounded.

NURSE BARTON: The bravery and kindness of one of the war's nurses soon became legendary. She was a short woman with dark, soulful eyes, and she went from battlefield to battlefield, braving enemy fire. No matter what happened, this nurse stayed at her job, even as the doctors fled. In the chaos of battle, she often had to operate on the men herself.

The nurse's name was Clara Barton (1821–1912). Those men who lived never forgot her kindness. She would survive the war and go on to found the American Red Cross.

SPIES IN HOOP SKIRTS: Most of the spies in the Civil War were slaves. Desperate for the North to win and secure their freedom from bondage, men and women slaves helped whenever they could, risking their lives by passing on information to the Union army.

But there was also a lot of spying done by well-to-do white women. The large hoop skirts worn at the time proved useful for women who wanted to smuggle weapons, secret papers, and other contraband over the border to either the North or the South.

The most famous woman spy for the South was Belle Boyd, who was known as La Belle Rebelle and kept on with her spying despite six arrests. She once even managed to continue her activities from her jail cell, hiding coded secrets in

▲ *Grant, as the new head of the army, looks over General* Meade's shoulder as they study a map during a council of war, May 21, 1864.

This 15-inch shell gun was ▶ designed by John Adolphus Dahlgren (1809–70), who became chief of the Bureau of Ordnance (weapons) in 1862. His innovative designs revolutionized naval weaponry.

◀ *Sixty-third Ohio Volunteer Infantry, at Corinth. The men fired in lines, then moved back to reload.*

a rubber ball and tossing it out to a fellow spy.

The North, on the other hand, had Elizabeth Van Lew of Richmond. Van Lew had her friends and neighbors thinking she was just a silly old woman, but she was busily gathering information from one of Jefferson Davis's slaves and passing it on to the Union army.

DISGUISED AS MEN: Though women spies were given less severe punishments than men were, spying was still a dangerous job. But some women sought even more deadly work. It is believed that as many as 400 Northern women may have dressed up like men and sneaked their way into various battalions.

Women soldiers were a rare exception to the rule. But women were taking on men's roles in another way—and in large numbers. With so many men away at war, women worked the farms and stores, as well as cared for the children. They lived with the knowledge that many husbands would never return.

▲ *In terms of raw supplies, Northern victory seemed assured. Here, siege mortars and other matériel await use at Yorktown, Virginia.*

▼ *A reenactment. In the Civil War, men used muzzle-loading rifles and had to reload under fire. A man's mistake could be fatal to those around him.*

▲ *Union guns at Stones River, Tennessee, 1862. (Some Union divisions wore gray.)*

A sharpshooter of the Army ▶ *of the Potomac on guard duty using a telescopic sight. His uniform is a special camouflage green.*

The Struggle for Vicksburg

In the east, Lincoln was trying general after general—without finding anyone who could stop Lee. In the meantime, war in the west had bogged down as well.

Farragut's courageous naval assault had won New Orleans, but the South still had control of the strategic port of Vicksburg. The North had been trying to take the city since the autumn of 1862. For Union forces in the west, Vicksburg had become the one and only goal.

SHIPS CAN'T CRAWL: Farragut's fleet tried but couldn't help them. Vicksburg was nestled atop hills 300 feet high. As Farragut said, his ships couldn't crawl uphill.

William Tecumseh Sherman (1820–91) tried next, with land forces. He fought his way to the city but could find no way to take the enemy positions high on the hills.

Then, in January 1863, Grant arrived with 45,000 soldiers. They would try a new approach.

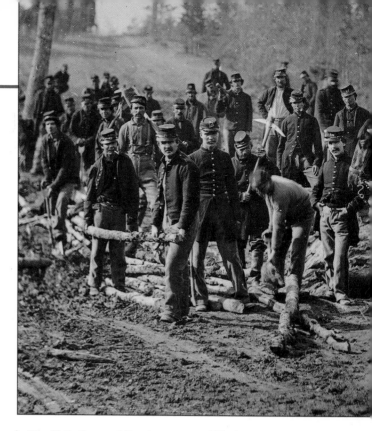

▲ *The U.S. Corps of Engineers had the crucial task of building—and rebuilding—roads and bridges. They did their work with astonishing speed.*

▼ *The U.S. Military Railroad's Fred Leach. With fuel scarce, wood-burning trains like these helped the Northern cause.*

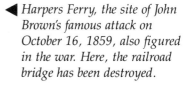

◀ *Harpers Ferry, the site of John Brown's famous attack on October 16, 1859, also figured in the war. Here, the railroad bridge has been destroyed.*

▼ *Union engineers constructing telegraph lines in April 1864. Thanks to these lines, generals could wire information to Washington.*

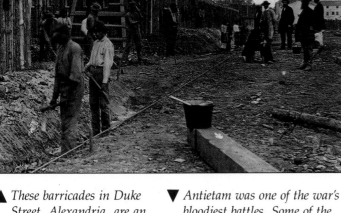

▲ *These barricades in Duke Street, Alexandria, are an attempt to protect the Union railroad from Confederate cavalry raiders.*

▼ *Antietam was one of the war's bloodiest battles. Some of the worst fighting occurred as General Burnside tried to lead the North over this bridge.*

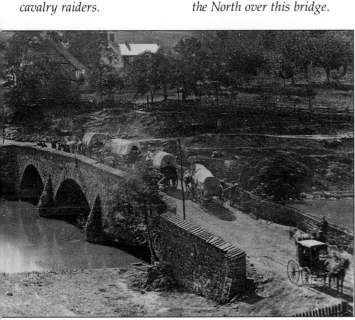

For months, he and his men attempted to cut their way through the swamps and take the hills of Vicksburg from the other side.

The swamps themselves stopped the Yankee attack. The men just could not make it through.

BAD PRESS: Early victories had made Grant a hero, but now, as his attack faltered, Northern newspapers demanded that he be fired. Grant had once had a drinking problem. It was rumored that he was drinking again.

But then, Grant hit on a daring scheme. He would cross the Mississippi south of Vicksburg, travel into enemy territory, cut his army off from supplies, and try to fight his way back to the hilly city from behind.

Even Sherman, who was known for his boldness, thought the plan was too risky. But Grant went ahead. And in late March, his army began to move.

Gettysburg

Winning battle after battle, Grant's men fought their way back to Vicksburg, surrounded the city from the rear, and began a siege.

Jefferson Davis met with Lee. They knew that Vicksburg could not hold out forever. Davis wanted to send reinforcements. But the Confederate army had few men to spare. As usual, Lee's plan was daring and surprising. He proposed that they attack, marching north to Washington. If they came close enough to the Union capital, Grant and his army would have to leave Vicksburg and come to the rescue.

Lincoln had named yet another general to head the Army of the Potomac, George Gordon Meade (1815–72). Meade and his massive army headed north to cut off Lee.

Neither army was exactly sure where the other one was located. Then the two armies bumped into each other, at the tiny town of Gettysburg.

THE BIGGEST BATTLE OF ALL: The rebels had come to the town because it was rumored to hold a supply of shoes—and shoes were scarce among the rebs. Instead, they found federal cavalry.

Both sides quickly called for reinforcements. On the first day, the

▼ *A rebel tends a muzzle-loading cannon on the Confederate gunboat* Teaser, *1862.*

▲ *After the success of the* Monitor, *the North built more iron ships, like this one, the* Sangamon. *Even the deck was made of armor plate.*

The Maratanza *floats on the* ▶
James *on July 4, 1862, after
capturing the Confederate
Teaser.*

▼ *Engineers build a pontoon
bridge during the battle at
Fredericksburg.*

▼ *Ironclads helped the North
in its relentless artillery
attacks on Mississippi
forts.*

rebels pushed the Yankees back, all the way to Cemetery Ridge.

It would have been a good position for the Union soldiers to defend, except for one thing. There were hills looking down on the Union soldiers on either side. Much of the second day would be spent fighting over those hills.

Somehow, 350 Maine soldiers under Joshua Chamberlain managed to hold one hill, Little Round Top, against several thousand rebels. For his valor, Chamberlain would win the congressional Medal of Honor.

PICKETT'S CHARGE: The fighting would last for three hellish days. Sometimes the two armies were only a few feet apart as soldiers fired directly into each other's faces. The third day, Lee made what may have been his only mistake of the war. He ordered General George E. Pickett (1825–75) to lead an assault against the center of the Union line. It was the same mistake Burnside had made at Marye's Heights. For half of Pickett's men, Lee's mistake meant death.

Needed: More Men!

Though both sides suffered terrible losses, Gettysburg was still a victory for the North. Lee's advance had been stopped cold, and he also had lost several thousand more men than the North had. With his smaller army, he couldn't afford to lose anyone.

Lee's plan to save Vicksburg was another casualty at Gettysburg. Since Grant didn't have to worry about defending his own capital, he was able to maintain his death grip on the Mississippi port. The people of Vicksburg were starving, and every day, the Union forces lobbed in more shells. At last, on July 3, 1863, Vicksburg surrendered.

Lincoln saw a chance to end the whole war. He urged General Meade to follow up his attack and crush Lee once and for all. But Meade moved slowly. Once again, Lincoln's commander in the field frustrated the president with his caution.

THE DRAFT RIOTS: The South wasn't alone in its desperate need for soldiers. Lincoln's army needed reinforcements as well. And that summer, Lincoln instituted a draft for 300,000 new soldiers.

This cutaway drawing of ▶ the Confederate ship Alabama *reveals her internal machinery. For extra power, she has both sails and steam engines.*

A young "powder monkey" seen beside the gun he served. In the Civil War, thousands of young boys ▲ enlisted and served.

▼ The paddle steamer Giraffe *is being fitted out as a blockade-runner, the* Robert E. Lee.

Any man between the ages of 20 and 45 was eligible to be called. The names of those selected were posted in the newspapers.

Up until now, men had volunteered eagerly. But Northern support for Lincoln's long war had faded badly.

Lincoln had added a special rule to his draft to help raise money. Any man selected in the draft could buy his way out, for $300. The thought of rich men buying their way out of the service infuriated many poor people. Violent riots broke out in New York City. The rioters burned buildings and attacked blacks, whom they saw as the cause of the war.

In the end, troops had to be called away from the front to stop the uprising.

◀ A Union lieutenant commander holds a telescope to help watch for blockade-runners like the one pictured below.

▲ The crew members of the Mendota work on one of her massive guns.

▼ A Confederate blockade-runner cruises near Fort Monroe, Virginia, December 1864.

5 The Battle Turns *Black Troops Fight for Freedom*

After lynching and burning an innocent black man, draft rioters in New York City cheered for Jefferson Davis. Attacks such as these showed once again what Northern blacks had already known too well. They were free from slavery but not from prejudice.

There were many Southern sympathizers in the North who hated fighting to end slavery, hated fighting the blacks' war.

Northern blacks hated that idea as well. Since the beginning of the war, they had been clamoring for the right to fight for themselves.

At first Lincoln had said no. He was struggling to keep more Southern states from seceding, and he knew that many whites would refuse to fight alongside blacks.

TO ARMS!: It wasn't until 1863 that Northern blacks were at last allowed to enlist. They rushed to join up in record numbers.

▲ *It all began here, at Fort Sumter, where Major Robert Anderson needed many more large guns like this one, to hold off the rebels. It took years for the Union to retake the fort.*

▼ *The Confederates charge at the first battle of Bull Run on July 21, 1861. The Union men, on the right, are about to run in what they later called the Great Skedaddle.*

Black soldiers were kept in all-black troops, could not rise to become officers (their officers were all white), and were given poor equipment and uniforms, if any at all. Frederick Douglass, the escaped slave and brilliant orator, went to Washington and complained to President Lincoln in person. Sadly, Lincoln said it was the best he could do for now.

THE 54TH LEADS THE CHARGE: For years, Southerners had been saying that black people were inferior to whites. It was a way of justifying slavery, and the idea had sunk in in the North as well. Few believed that black troops would amount to anything or that blacks could possibly be as brave as white soldiers.

The all-black 54th Massachusetts Regiment was the first of many black troops to see heavy action. The men knew that the eyes of the nation were upon them.

On July 18, the regiment led an impossible charge up the hill to Fort Wagner in South Carolina. Almost half of the brave troops were killed.

When the order to retreat was finally given, the color bearer (who carried the flag) lay dead. One of the black soldiers, William Carney, rushed to retrieve the flag. He was shot four times but didn't stop until he had carried it back to his lines.

▲ *The Union was winning the first Bull Run battle when General Barnard E. Bee (rear) pointed to Thomas Jackson. "Look, there is Jackson standing like a stone wall. Rally behind the Virginians!"*

▲ *The opening shots are fired at Boonville, Missouri. Fighting for control of the state, Union troops at Boonville were able to rout the Missouri militia.*

◀ *There was often nothing the men could do to help their wounded comrades. Here, soldiers carry their wounded general from the field at Ball's Bluff.*

The Gettysburg Address

For months, it had seemed as if the North was just about to land the decisive blow and finally end the war. But that blow never came. Fighting seesawed back and forth, with heavy losses on both sides. The mood of the nation was grim, as more and more blood was shed.

November 19, 1863, was not a happy day for President Lincoln. The Union was holding a ceremony to dedicate a vast new military cemetery at Gettysburg, where so many men had recently fallen.

President Lincoln and his secretary of state rode out on a special train from Washington. On the trip, Lincoln scrawled notes for his speech on the back of an envelope.

A crowd of close to 6,000 gathered for the event. The main speaker was Edward Everett, who was known for his powers of oratory.

Everett spoke for almost two hours. Then Lincoln got up.

THEY *WILL* REMEMBER: Lincoln did not have a powerful speaking voice (it was said to be high and toneless). He spoke for only two minutes. There was only polite applause. One reporter wrote that Lincoln's speech had made the whole ceremony "ludicrous."

But today, no one knows or remembers what Everett said. Lincoln's brief speech—just 293 words—has become one of the most famous in the world. Here is what he said:

▲ *General McClellan hands over command of the Army of the Potomac to General Burnside (right).*

▼ *At Malvern Hill, well-placed Union batteries drive off Lee's attack and inflict heavy losses.*

▲ *This map of the Antietam battlefield is based on a Union engineer's survey.*

This Union cavalry charge ▶ *was part of the campaign that led to the second Bull Run.*

▼ *At Fredericksburg, Union infantry wait to join the battle.*

Fourscore and seven years ago our fathers brought forth on this continent a new nation, conceived in liberty and dedicated to the proposition that all men are created equal.

Now we are engaged in a great civil war, testing whether that nation or any nation so conceived and so dedicated can long endure. We are met on a great battle field of that war. We have come to dedicate a portion of that field, as a final resting-place for those who here gave their lives that that nation might live. It is altogether fitting and proper that we should do this.

But, in a larger sense, we can not dedicate—we can not consecrate—we can not hallow—this ground. The brave men, living and dead, who struggled here, have consecrated it, far above our poor power to add or detract. The world will little note, nor long remember, what we say here, but it can never forget what they did here. It is for us the living, rather, to be dedicated here to the unfinished work which they who fought here have thus far so nobly advanced. It is rather for us to be here dedicated to the great task remaining before us—that from these honored dead we take increased devotion to that cause for which they gave the last full measure of devotion—that we here highly resolve that these dead shall not have died in vain—that this nation, under God, shall have a new birth of freedom—and that government of the people, by the people, for the people, shall not perish from the earth.

Lincoln Turns to Grant

On paper at least, Northern victory seemed inevitable. The North's rich, manufacturing economy kept pumping money, weapons, and men into the war effort. The Union army was larger, better equipped, better fed. So why couldn't the North stop the South's secession once and for all?

For three years, President Lincoln had searched for an officer who could find a way to win. Now he decided to try one last time. The man he turned to was Ulysses S. Grant.

FROM CLERK TO GENERAL-IN-CHIEF: Before the war began, Grant had been at home in Galena, Illinois, working as a clerk in his father's leather store. He was so broke he had had to pawn his watch to buy Christmas presents for his wife and children. Beginning on March 2, 1864, the short, bearded man would lead the entire Union army.

Grant organized the vast Union forces into four main armies that would each attack part of the Confederacy. He gave his old friend Sherman the assignment of attacking Atlanta. He himself would join with General Meade in fighting the Union's greatest foe, Robert E. Lee. Once Lee's army had been destroyed, the troops would move on to take Richmond.

Grant was known among his men for his steely determination. He promised that the Union army would not turn back. This time they would get the job done.

INTO THE WILDERNESS: As Grant's men moved south, they sometimes camped on old battlefields, amid the skulls and bones of fallen comrades. It was an ominous beginning. The fighting began in a stretch of woods known as the Wilderness. Day after day, the two armies clashed as Grant tried repeatedly to move around Lee's right flank. One night, men heard him weeping in his tent. In 30 days of fighting, he had lost 50,000 men, and he still had not defeated Lee.

◄ *Confederates retreat after the war's second great battle, Shiloh.*

▲ *General Smith's division charges during the fall of Fort Donelson, Tennessee.*

Captain Bailey faces a hostile crowd as he lands on New Orleans's levee under a flag of truce. He demanded the city surrender to the federal government. General Mansfield Lovell refused.

▲ As Memphis's citizens helplessly watch, Union wooden rams shatter the River Defense Fleet offshore.

◀ Northern illustration of the battle of Corinth (October 3–4, 1862). Its caption proudly claims the rebs were "utterly defeated and driven from the field." In truth, the battle was close to a draw.

▼ General Carlin made a name for himself leading the infantry in Missouri and a brigade in Tennessee, notably at Stones River. Here, he stands with staff, in 1863.

The Endless Siege of Petersburg

After such heavy losses, newspapers began calling Grant a butcher, and advisers pressed Lincoln to fire him. But Lincoln didn't give up on Grant. And Grant didn't give up, either.

His army had almost reached Richmond. He started to move toward the Confederate capital.

Lee quickly moved his army to block Grant.

But Grant was bluffing. And for once, Lee was fooled. Grant now moved his forces to Petersburg, a city just outside of Richmond. If Grant could control this city, he would cut off Richmond's access to supplies. Eventually, Grant hoped, the capital would be forced to surrender.

ANOTHER COSTLY DELAY: Moving a large army is a hard process. Grant's troops didn't arrive in Petersburg all at once. But the first troops—16,000 of them—got to Petersburg way before Lee. They were facing only 3,000 rebels. But the Union general in charge, W. F. "Baldy" Smith, refused to attack. He insisted on waiting for the rest of Grant's army. By the time Grant got there, rebel reinforcements had arrived as well. Another precious opportunity had been lost.

Now there was nothing to do but settle in

▲ *Union troops storm over Missionary Ridge, a turning point in the Chattanooga battle.*

▼ *Grant and his three generals watch the battle at Chattanooga—one of his greatest tactical victories. His victories here and at Vicksburg broke rebel power in the west.*

for a long siege. Grant ordered his men to dig trenches. Throughout the siege, his men would have to live in these hot, open ditches.

Grant was determined to wait it out and slowly strangle the city. But one of his generals had a plan for speeding up the attack. Using a regiment of coal miners, General Burnside dug a huge tunnel toward enemy lines and stuffed it with gunpowder. His idea was to blast a hole in the enemy lines and rush through it into the city. The huge explosion cost many lives, and it left a huge crater. But Burnside didn't get his surprise attack started for another hour. And when he did charge, his men got stuck in the crater, as the Confederates fired down upon them.

Grant's siege continued. It would last for ten miserable months.

▲ The Union captioned this scene of the Chancellorsville disaster: "The brave Union soldiers fought with desperate gallantry, holding the rebels in check and inflicting dreadful slaughter."

▼ Stonewall Jackson, about to be shot by his own men, in the confusion of battle. His death was a serious loss to the Southern cause.

◄ Admiral Farragut's ships brave heavy fire as they pass Port Hudson's batteries on their way to Vicksburg.

▼ During the battle at Chickamauga, Lieutenant Van Pelt defends his field battery.

Lincoln Fights for His Office

The war had stretched into 1864, its fourth year. That year was also an election year. Things did not look good for President Lincoln.

Northerners were fed up with the endless war, and they blamed their president. Lincoln vowed to fight on to victory, but victory appeared to be nowhere in sight. He and advisers felt his chances of being reelected were close to zero.

Unless.

Unless the Union could win a major victory that would make the end of the war seem close.

A CITY ON FIRE: Instead, there were more losses. Jubal Anderson Early, the Confederate cavalry raider, held hostage the entire

General G. E. Pickett's ill-fated charge at Gettysburg is among the most famous episodes in military history. It cost Pickett 7,000 of his 15,000 men. The assault's failure ended the battle

Burying Union dead after ▶ Gettysburg. This part of the battle, nicknamed Devil's Den, was one of many sites that saw tremendous fighting.

◀ Lincoln's Gettysburg Address was so brief that photographers didn't have time to capture the moment. Barely noticed then, his speech has been hailed as one of the greatest ever.

Confederates taken at ▶ Gettysburg show the South's lack of uniforms. In fact, the Gettysburg battle began because the Southern forces heard there was a supply of shoes at Gettysburg.

This engraving of the hand-to-hand fighting at Gettysburg captures some of the violent confusion of infantry warfare. At such close quarters, men had to use their rifles as clubs.

▲ The brave men in Pickett's charge reached the Union line only once. Every Confederate who came over the wall was killed or taken prisoner.

city of Chambersburg, Pennsylvania. If the townspeople refused to pay his men $500,000, he said he would burn down the town. They did refuse, and Early scorched the city.

LITTLE MAC RETURNS AGAIN: To run against Lincoln, the Democrats nominated the general who had cost Lincoln so many early battles: George McClellan. The Democrats promised the country they would stop the war and make peace with the South.

"I am going to be beaten," Lincoln predicted, "and unless some great change takes place, *badly* beaten."

There seemed only one ray of hope. Sherman's army was having some success in its quest to take Atlanta, steadily driving back the Confederate forces under Joseph E. Johnston.

Then, on August 31, the news came.

Atlanta Falls

The headlines cried victory. Sherman had captured Atlanta, a key Southern city.

Still dug in outside of Petersburg, Grant ordered his men to fire their guns in salute.

Grant would have reason to fire the guns again soon. In September, another branch of his army, under General Philip Henry Sheridan (1831–88), defeated Jubal Early's raiders and retook control of the Shenandoah Valley.

Early's surprise attacks had plagued the North for years. The Union had finally stopped him.

HOLDING ON: By now, the North's naval blockade had destroyed the South's cotton business. All over the Confederacy, food was scarce. So was money, and prices were soaring. A barrel of flour now sold for as much as $425!

The South's strategy had come down to this—try to hold on. The North was tired of fighting. If the Confederacy could keep from surrendering, and if they could inflict more damage on Union troops, then maybe McClellan and the peace ticket would be elected. The North would compromise. The South could rejoin the Union but keep their slaves.

HOW WILL THE SOLDIERS VOTE?: November came, and the election drew near. Just a few months before, Lincoln had seemed to have no chance of winning the election or the war. But Sherman and Sheridan had changed that. Now the end of war was in sight. Maybe Northerners would let him finish the task he had set for himself—holding the Union together. One big question remained: How will the soldiers vote?

After all, Lincoln's chief opponent was a former general, one the men had worshiped. Lincoln knew that out of caution, or possibly even cowardice, General McClellan had cost the lives of thousands of soldiers. But the soldiers didn't know that.

After the voting, Lincoln was tense as he waited for the returns. He needn't have worried. Union soldiers didn't want the North to make peace. That would have been the same as admitting defeat. Seventy-eight percent of the forces voted for Abe.

Lincoln could finish the war.

▲ *Col. Addison W. Preston led his First Vermont Cavalry in General Custer's decisive charge against Jeb Stuart.*

At Cold Harbor, Virginia, ▶ *on June 1, 1864, the North advanced. In the first eight minutes of this infamous charge, 7,000 Union fell.*

▼ *Grant urges on his troops during one of the bloody assaults on Lee's army during the Wilderness campaign.*

▲ *Even the heaviest Union artillery—including this 2,000-pound mortar—failed to break Petersburg.*

▼ *Philip Sheridan (third from left), the cavalry general who finally stopped Jubal Early. The victory helped keep Lincoln in office.*

Sherman's March

When the Confederate forces gave up Atlanta to Sherman, they blew up factories and other buildings rather than let them fall into Northern hands. Sherman's men finished the job, demolishing train stations and setting fire to a third of the city. By the time both sides were done, Atlanta had been destroyed.

Sherman had no second thoughts about destroying the town. He believed that part of his job was to discourage Southern civilians so that they would give up the fight. He wanted to wipe out crops and any other supplies that could help his enemy.

EVERYTHING IN HIS PATH: To accomplish these goals, Sherman and his army now set out for the coast. His plan was to march straight through Georgia, all the way to Savannah, wreaking destruction on everything in his path.

He would be cut off from his supplies. But supplies would be plentiful on this march, for Sherman ordered his men to steal whatever food they needed from the Southern plantations they marched across.

By now, a terrible famine had spread throughout the South. But wherever they went, Sherman's army emptied what was left in the larders. And what the men couldn't eat themselves, they burned.

At each plantation, slaves ran to join the conquering army. Carrying their children in their

▲ *An Atlanta street, in 1864, before Sherman captured, and razed, the town. Sherman's* *Atlanta victory was one of the death knells of the Confederacy.*

▲ *On Kennesaw Mountain, Sherman's men assault a heavily fortified rebel position.*

◄ *Sherman's troops destroy train tracks in Atlanta, a city that served as the junction of four major Southern railroads. The soldiers bent the rails in half in what were called "Sherman's hairpins."*

A very mild-looking Northern view of Sherman's violent march to the sea. The march covered 425 miles and destroyed everything in its path.

One of Sherman's wagons ▶ crossing a river. For wide rivers, his engineers threw together quick bridges out of pontoons— flat-bottomed boats.

▼ Even the ironclad Tennessee failed to stop Farragut's fleet. Here, she engages his flagship before Union ironclads attack and overcome her.

▲ Admiral Farragut's fleet was crucial in helping the North. Farragut himself is one of the most distinguished officers in U.S. history.

arms, barefoot men and women ran after the Union wagons, praying that the Union men would protect them and set them free. By the end of Sherman's march, 25,000 slaves were following along behind his army. But Sherman had no interest in freeing slaves. He had never been strongly opposed to slavery and saw the grateful crowd as a nuisance. His only interest was in winning the war.

A COSTLY FIRE: He let his troops run wild. For years, these men had been living under the threat of death. Now here was a chance to get get revenge on the enemy, and they needed no encouragement.

The men shot farmers' pigs and cows. They set houses on fire. They molested the slave women.

In Milledgeville, the state capital, the soldiers gathered together all the Confederate money they could find, set it on fire, and roasted their coffee over the flames.

The South didn't have the troops to stop them. By the time Sherman reached Savannah, his men had destroyed $100 million worth of property.

They weren't through. Sherman now turned his march north, into South Carolina. South Carolina had been the first state to secede. In the eyes of Sherman and his men, the state was responsible for all the trouble, all the lost lives. And Sherman vowed that his next march would be even more violent than his last.

The Confederacy had made it into a new year. But it was on its last legs.

Grant's siege was starving both Petersburg and Richmond, just as he had hoped. Without food or clothes and facing bitter cold, Lee's barefoot men were deserting in large numbers.

Sherman had captured Columbia, the capital of South Carolina. As the rebels retreated, they set fire to a store of cotton to keep it from Sherman's men. The fire spread and burned another Southern city to the ground.

THE NATION'S WOUNDS: On March 4, 1865, Lincoln was sworn into office for a second term. "Let us strive on to finish the work we are in, to bind up the nation's wounds," he said in his speech.

One of the people in the crowd that day was a well-known actor, John Wilkes Booth. Booth was a passionate supporter of slavery. He hated Lincoln for setting the slaves free. From where he was standing, he said later, he had "an excellent chance . . . to kill the President."

LEE STRETCHES: Grant knew that Lee's army in Petersburg was growing weaker, and smaller, every day. So he kept building more trenches, extending the line of his forces to the left. To defend himself, Lee had to keep extending his line as well, to prevent the Union forces from charging around his flank.

But by now, 60,000 of Lee's men had deserted. He had only 35,000 soldiers left. And his line was stretching thinner and thinner. Grant had extended the trenches around Petersburg for 53 miles. Lee's men were standing farther and farther apart. Any day now, Lee knew, Grant would attack through one of the gaps.

Lee sent word to Jefferson Davis. When President Davis read his message, he turned gray. "My lines are broken in three places," Lee told him. "Richmond must be evacuated this evening." There was no choice. Davis and his government fled.

Lee pulled his troops out of Petersburg and rushed to join J. E. Johnston's army in North Carolina. But Grant was hard on his heels.

Union forces also stormed into Richmond. At 8:00 A.M. on April 3, soldiers ripped down the Confederate flag from the capital building and put the Union flag back in place. Still, Lee did not give up.

Federal soldiers pose with a wrecked locomotive after the fall of Richmond on April 3, 1865. ◀

Richmond in flames. The ▶ *Confederate forces had evacuated Petersburg and Richmond, and the government had fled.*

▼ *Outside Petersburg on July 30, 1864, Burnside's scheme backfired. He hoped that his gunpowder-filled tunnel would blow a hole in enemy lines. Instead, his men found themselves trapped in the giant crater left by the bomb.*

◀ *General Philip Sheridan rides his famous horse, Rienzi, as he and his men trap Lee's fleeing troops at Five Forks, Virginia.*

▲ *Robert E. Lee formally surrenders to Grant, whose terms are generous. He gives the rebels food and promises that soldiers who lay down their arms are free to go home.*

▼ *President Lincoln was with his wife and friends in a private box at Ford's Theatre, Washington, when actor John Wilkes Booth shot him. Lincoln's death rocked the nation.*

▲ *Famous war photographer Mathew B. Brady took this photograph of Lee in a new gray general's uniform soon after surrendering at Appomattox.*

6 The Final Act

ee's men struggled west, trying to escape Grant's army. Lee's own army desperately needed food. Lee had sent word to his country's war department to have rations—thousands of them—waiting for his men at Amelia Court House. His instructions never arrived. The rebels made it to Amelia Court House, but there was no food waiting.

The soldiers continued west, gnawing on dried corn—their own horses' food. Grant's well-fed troops, all 125,000 of them, drew closer.

THE LAST BATTLE: There would be more fighting. At Sayler's Creek, the Union finally caught up. Vastly outnumbered, Lee and his men fought with their last ounces of strength. They managed to avoid defeat. But the battle claimed 8,000 of Lee's starving men.

The next evening, a messenger rode into Lee's camp at Appomattox with a message from Grant. "The result of last week must convince you of the hopelessness of further resistance," Grant wrote. He asked Lee to surrender.

Instead, Lee met with his men and planned a

▼ *This photograph—entitled "Amputation in a hospital tent, Gettysburg, 1863"—was posed, but it does show the horrors of Civil War medicine. Wounded limbs were cut off with a saw.*

▼ *A war news vendor. The government, which controlled the telegraph lines, put restrictions on what news reached the papers.*

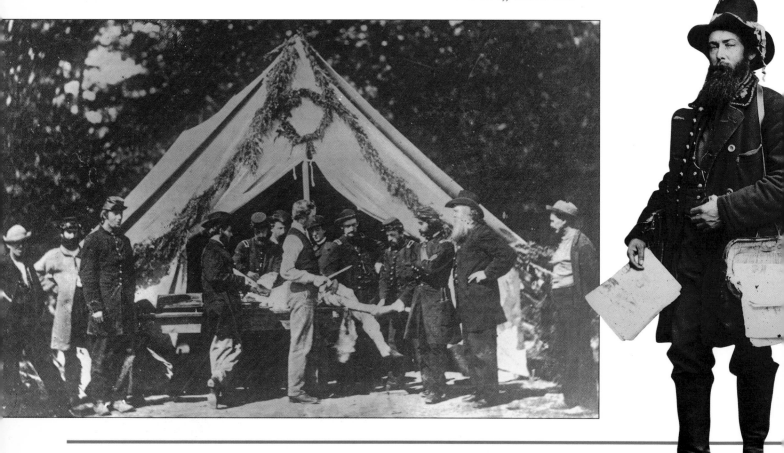

Dead Union soldiers—only one of them older than 25. Their boots and equipment have already been taken by soldiers who still need them.

▲ *New York* Herald *reporters watch the war. With more than 150 war correspondents for Northern papers alone, battles were well covered.*

▲ *One of the last to die. A young Confederate lies unburied at Fort Mahone in front of the abandoned city of Petersburg.*

▼ *The lucky survivors in this ward in Carver General Hospital, Washington, include several amputees.*

desperate maneuver for breaking out of the Union's clutches. The next morning, his men drove the Union cavalry back. But then Lee saw what was coming at him—and what was behind him. He was utterly surrounded by Grant's enormous army.

THE BEGINNING AND THE END: Lee sent a message to Grant. He would meet Grant to set the terms of surrender.

The house the soldiers chose for the generals' meeting belonged to an old farmer, Wilmer McLean. McLean's first house had been smack in the middle of Bull Run. He had moved south to avoid further trouble. But the war had caught up with him again. Said McLean, "The war began in my front yard and ended in my front parlor."

At the meeting, Grant offered to give the starving rebel troops food and promised that if they lay down their arms, they could go home free. Lee agreed, and both generals signed the treaty. As Lee rode back to his camp, his head hung low. His soldiers began to weep.

A Cowardly "Hero"

The war was finally over. The Union had been saved. In Washington, fireworks erupted, and a crowd gathered on the lawn of the White House. Lincoln was too exhausted to talk. Instead, he asked the band to play "Dixie," the Confederacy's anthem, in honor of the South. Visibly aged by his four difficult years in office, Lincoln could finally relax.

On Friday, April 14, he and his wife, Mary, went to Ford's Theatre to see a production of a British comedy entitled *Our American Cousin*. General Grant and his wife were supposed to join them but canceled at the last minute.

The Lincolns were sitting in special box seats, holding hands as they enjoyed the show. At the same time, an actor named John Wilkes Booth was making his way to the president's box.

In his own twisted thinking, Booth believed that Lincoln had to be stopped. He was convinced that Lincoln had secret plans to become more than president—a dictator, say, or a king. Booth had never found the courage to enlist during the war. He hoped that by his next act, he would finally become a hero.

Sic semper tyrannis: Booth shot Lincoln point-blank in the back of the head. Then he jumped down to the stage, breaking his leg in the fall, and shouted to the crowd. Some of the stunned

◀ *Photographed by a colleague, two photographers have a picnic lunch, complete with wine, in the Bull Run area, before the second battle, August 29, 1862.*

▲ *Mathew B. Brady (1823–96), the war's best-known photographer, was actually close to blind. Most of the photos were taken by his assistants, Alexander Gardner and Timothy O'Sullivan.*

◀ *Brady's artists use a mobile film-processing wagon. These men risked their lives to photograph the war.*

Waud's charcoal drawing of ▶ Burnside's "Mud March" (January 1863) captures the misery of winter campaigns.

▲ In addition to photographers, the war was covered by artists such as Henry Lovie, who made this on-the-spot sketch of Union troops storming a ford at Stones River.

Artist Alfred R. Waud made this rough charcoal sketch of the rebel Virginia cavalry during the Antietam campaign.

audience thought the man yelled, "Sic semper tyrannis," meaning "Thus be it ever to tyrants." Then the assassin limped off. He would die 12 days later, after having been cornered by federal troops.

Soldiers carried the wounded and unconscious president across the street to a boardinghouse. They had to lay the tall man sideways to fit him onto the bed. Lincoln's wife was sobbing helplessly, begging her husband to speak to her. He never did. The next morning, at 7:22 A.M., Abraham Lincoln died.

THE NATION MOURNS: The nation was rocked by the news. No president had ever been killed before. It was hard to believe. Thousands upon thousands poured out to watch Lincoln's long funeral procession—and to mourn.

Rebuilding the Nation

Peace did not bring quick relief. The war had been terribly costly.

In pure dollars, the Civil War cost well over $3 billion, for the North alone. But the North's economy was strong enough to survive. In fact, some say that the war effort—the need to churn out all those supplies and weapons—helped make Northern industry even stronger.

The Southern economy, on the other hand, was reeling.

IF LINCOLN HAD LIVED: President Lincoln believed that the North needed to treat the defeated South with care and help get it back on its feet. He also believed that the government should help the freed slaves so that they would truly become full citizens.

But Lincoln didn't live. And his plans were not carried out. In 1866, after a bitter political struggle, the 14th Amendment to the Constitution was passed, giving full citizenship to all black Americans and allowing them to vote for the first time. But under presidents such as Rutherford B. Hayes, the government looked the other way as the South ignored the amendment.

▲ We will never know what Abraham Lincoln would have gone on to do if he had lived.

▲ Jefferson Davis spent two years in jail for treason. He lived to be 81 and died believing in the right of Southern states to keep slaves.

Andrew Johnson succeeded ▶ Lincoln as president but didn't continue Lincoln's policies of helping blacks and the defeated South.

◀ In 1876, a convention was held in Tennessee, to fight for black rights. The Ku Klux Klan, a group of anti-black terrorists, began here in 1867.

▲ *An 1860s woodcut shows black Americans celebrating the end of slavery.*

The First Vote, as drawn ▶ by A. R. Waud in 1867, shows former slaves going to the polls in the first state election after the war.

Blacks were free but still far from equal in civil rights. And it would remain for people such as Martin Luther King, Jr., a century later in the 1960s, to finish what Lincoln had begun.

But the Civil War *had* taken a huge step forward. Slavery had finally ended, and the nation had remained whole.

Further Reading about the Civil War

If you want to read more about the Civil War, you're in luck. More than 50,000 books have been written on the subject!

After you've read through everything at your local library, here are some titles you'll be able to find—or order—at a bookstore:

American Heritage Illustrated History of the United States. Vol. 8. *The Civil War.* New York: Choice Publications, 1988.

Canon, Jill. *Civil War Heroines.* Santa Barbara, Calif.: Bellerophon Books, 1989.

Dubowski, Cathy E. *Clara Barton: Healing the Wounds.* Englewood Cliffs, N.J.: Silver Burdett Press, 1990.

Fritz, Jean. *Stonewall.* New York: G. P. Putnam's Sons, 1979.

McPherson, James M. *Marching Toward Freedom: Blacks in the Civil War, 1861–1865.* New York: Facts on File, 1990.

Ray, Delia. *Behind the Blue and Gray: The Soldier's Life in the Civil War.* New York: E. P. Dutton, 1991.

Voices from the Civil War: A Documentary History of the Great American Conflict. New York: HarperCollins, 1989.

Picture Credits

The publishers would like to thank the picture agencies and individual collectors who supplied the photographs reproduced in this book. Special thanks are due to John Batchelor, Bert Campbell, Ronnie Nichols, Lisle Reedstrom, and Professor Gregory Urwin, who supplied pictures from their personal archives. Pictures are credited by page numbers.

J. Batchelor: 26 upper artwork, 27 artwork, 40–41 artwork. **The Bettmann Archive:** title page, 4–5, 6–7, 8 lower, 9 upper and middle, 10, 10–11, 11 top, middle left and right, 12 lower left, 13 upper, 14–15, 16, 17, 18, 19 upper left and right, 20–21, 22 middle and lower, 23 upper and lower right, 24 lower left, 25 upper, 26 middle, 26 lower left, 27 lower left, 28 lower left, 28–29, 30–31 upper, 31 lower right, 34 upper, 35 upper and lower, 36–37, 37 upper, 38–39 lower, 40, 41 middle right, 42 lower, 43 upper, middle, and lower, 44–45, 46 lower left and right, 46–47, 47 upper and middle, 48 upper and lower, 48–49 upper and lower, 49 lower, 50 middle left and right, and lower, 51 upper and lower, 52–53 upper and lower, 53 upper, 54 middle and lower, 55, 56–57, 58 lower right, 59 upper right and middle, 60 upper middle, and lower, 62–63. **Colour Library Books**

Ltd: 8 upper, 9 lower, 12–13, 19 middle left, 29 upper left and right, 30–31 lower, 31 middle and lower left, 42 upper, 47 lower, 50 upper right, 61 middle right. **G.A.R. Memorial Hall Museum:** 25 lower (via G. Urwin). **Library of Congress:** 11 lower, 16–18–19, 23 lower left (via G. Urwin), 34–35, 38, 39 upper right, 41 middle left and lower right, 49 upper, 54 upper, 58–59, 61 upper, middle left, and lower. **Massachusetts Commandery:** 25 middle (via G. Urwin). **Military Archive and Research Services (MARS):** 12 lower right, 13 lower, 28 upper, 29 middle, 34 lower, 35 middle left, 36, 37 middle left, right, and lower, 39 middle. **National Archives, Washington, D.C.:** 2–3, 2 upper, 24–25 (via G. Urwin), 30 (via Bert Campbell), 38–39 upper, 52 upper right (via G. Urwin), 53 lower right (via G. Urwin), 58 lower left (via MARS), 59 lower right (via MARS). **Ronnie Nichols:** 24 lower right. **E. Lisle Reedstrom:** 27 lower right, 35 middle right. **Fran Stevens, The Design Shop:** 32–33 map. **U.S. Army Military History Institute:** 26 lower right (via G. Urwin). **U.S. Navy:** 40–41 lower.

Cover pictures: Bettmann Archive (front center, front lower left, back); National Archives/G. Urwin (front upper left); National Archives/Bert Campbell (front right).

Index